THE FORGOTTEN
VICTIM

THE FORGOTTEN VICTIM

Annie Owen

Book Guild Publishing
Sussex, England

First published in Great Britain in 2009 by
The Book Guild Ltd
Pavilion View
19 New Road
Brighton, BN1 1UF

Typesetting in Times by
Keyboard Services, Luton, Bedfordshire

Printed in Great Britain by
CPI Antony Rowe

A catalogue record for this book is available from
The British Library

ISBN 978 1 84624 329 5

This is my true story of actual events as they happened; some names have been changed.

I dedicate this book to my mother Margaret and father Jim for their great love and support. They have been my guiding stars. Also to Maria and Nicky who have supported me and been good friends throughout my life.

And a very special dedication to Police Constable Squires, who sadly died shortly after the attack. He helped me and believed my story, and his advice and support have been a great inspiration to me.

Chapter 1

As the removal van pulled away a feeling of the unknown filled the air, we were leaving our old house in Stoke-on-Trent and moving to another county, Devon. A new house, new jobs and a new school were awaiting us.

As we passed by our neighbours they waved goodbye to us. It was a sad farewell. We were leaving behind a large family: my mother, one of eleven girls, had said goodbye to her sisters, her brothers-in-law who were like brothers to her, and her nieces and nephews. Our family were so close. My father too was leaving his four brothers and one sister.

Both families grew up together and had all worked with each other in the pottery industry after they finished school. Those were the only jobs available, working as a fettler, or a mould runner carrying long planks of wood on your shoulder, balancing numerous heavy pots and plates as you climbed a ladder to reach the top of the kiln. Breakages were commonplace and deductible from the meagre wages. Conditions were harsh, with no unions to protect the workers, no Human Rights, no Health and Safety. Breathing in their daily allowance of clay dust, they worked long hours for a weekly wage that today would not even buy the groceries.

My grandmother on my father's side ran the pottery

with a rod of iron. All my father's brothers and his sister worked there too, as did my mother and some of her sisters. According to the family, my grandmother was the quickest cup-maker in the business, a hard taskmaster. Her husband worked under her and she gave him no slack for being her husband; if anything he had the worst deal of all having his wife giving the orders. But she was a high earner in her day and the company knew they were on to a good thing with her. She drank two bottles of brown ale a night to keep her throat clear of the clay dust, chest and breathing problems were common within the industry.

At some point she developed cancer and had a major operation, and astonishingly she made a complete recovery. This was a miracle: treatment for cancer then was not advanced, and even today with all our expertise, drugs and knowledge it is still for some a terminal and fatal illness, with maybe a five-year term of remission where for a few this illness comes back to haunt them.

For a while when my parents were courting (what a lovely word that is to describe a relationship) my grandmother did not approve, as my father in her eyes was a god and no woman was good enough for him. She mellowed with time after my parents married, and she was always very kind to my mother.

I used to visit her on Saturday mornings and she would make me dripping sandwiches, I remember her pale blue glasses and her white hair, she was the only grandparent I ever met – all the others were already dead when I was born. But sadly she died a few months after we moved.

After a few hours on the road my father indicated left and pulled over onto the verge. In those days when cars and other motor vehicles were not so numerous on our roads, the verge was always used as a rest stop. He got out of the car and opened the boot, then he proceeded to take out a portable gas stove, a frying pan, eggs and bacon, and set about cooking us a mouth-watering meal.

Food cooking outdoors always has an irresistible smell; there is nothing quite like eggs and bacon by the roadside, indoor cooking just does not have the same appeal or flavour.

After lunch we set off again. I was wondering how long it would take to get to our new house. I must have fallen asleep, and was woken by Dad saying, 'Look, Devon'. I looked out of the window and there was a large sign by the roadside welcoming us to this beautiful, unspoilt county which was to be our new home.

The scenery was breathtaking, rolling hills and meadows full of wild flowers, farmers harvesting their crops, the smell of hay in the hot sunshine travelled on the breeze.

Chapter 2

Eventually we arrived at a small town called Dawlish. Even today its population is only about 15,000.

We pulled up in front of a row of nine large Georgian houses – ours was Number 1. It was an impressive structure: out of all the houses in the row this was the grandest and it had the biggest front door I had ever seen. A veranda ran the length of the frontage, and the garden had a tropical feel with its mature palm trees.

My parents had visited Dawlish many times as two of my mother's sisters had also left Stoke-on-Trent to start new lives here. If it was a rainy day, visitors would visit the local estate agents who would give them a handful of keys; they were all unaccompanied viewings, so when you had browsed and explored you would simply take the keys back to the agent. On a recent trip to the town my parents viewed the house, and fell in love with it.

We had purchased the house with an elderly sitting tenant who occupied the top floor of the house; this was a way of securing a property much more cheaply, and eventually if the tenant moved or died you would then have full occupancy of the house.

My mother knocked loudly on the door and after several minutes a large lady opened it. She was a South

African lady called Mrs Dade, and she informed us that the door was open – we only had to turn the knob!

I ran into the large hallway. The ceiling was so high, and the sunlight was streaming through a large window. A musty smell indicated that it had been several years since any windows had been opened. You could get lost for years in this house, I remember thinking to myself.

My parents had taken a gamble in life, left their jobs and sold their home to move to a new community with no jobs and no income. It was a brave decision to make, but sometimes you have to take a few risks in life. There was no doubt that this house had much potential, and my parents always had an eye for quality and a bargain.

After a couple of weeks my father got a job, and during the evenings and weekends he would work to refurbish and restore the house to its former glory. Within a few short months most of the seven bedrooms were finished. My father was a perfectionist, a craftsman with a precision hand. He had no formal qualifications, but his decorating skills and finishing touches were magnificent.

The lounge was a jewel, a large imposing room with two floor-to-ceiling sash windows, huge shutters on the inside, a highly polished marble fireplace, and a crystal chandelier. It was a tranquil room.

There was a large larder which still had meat hooks hanging from the ceiling, and in the kitchen was an ancient cooking range. A secret staircase was found hidden behind a wall.

The main staircase was very grand with its sweeping curve and carved banister, leading to elegant bedrooms all with marble fireplaces and ornate cornices.

The house builders of the day left their legacy of architectural brilliance in these houses, creating large rooms with high ceilings, so light and airy. Homes today are often too small to take furniture upstairs to the bedrooms. They have a kitchen where only one occupant at a time can work, and bedrooms that will only just fit your new bed.

Chapter 3

It was September 1971 and, aged five, I was enrolled in the primary school only a few streets away from my house. It was only a small class with about 15 pupils, and I made friends quickly. Children are always curious to meet someone new from another place, so for a while I was the main topic of conversation.

I could see why my parents had left Stoke-on-Trent; there could not be any better place to bring up children than wonderful Devon. Trips to Dartmoor in my father's green Ford Anglia showed me things I could only have dreamed of, an endless landscape of harsh and unforgiving terrain where wild ponies roamed free. It was heaven on earth to me. My only memory of Stoke was that it was always raining, grey and cold. Did the sun ever shine there?

I remember a hot Saturday when I was riding my purple scooter along the road from one end to the other – children were considered quite safe to play outside without fear of abduction or injury in those days. I decided to ride down the hill, and as I reached the bottom a girl on her yellow scooter rode over to me. Her name was Maria and she was also five – our birthdays were three days apart. She lived across the road above her parents' fish and chip shop. A lifelong friendship evolved from that chance meeting, and we became inseparable. There was a communal garden with our house where we would spend hours playing, enjoying daily picnics of sandwiches and crisps, exploring our safe haven.

In December, as we looked forward to our first Christmas in our new house, my father arrived home with news that a real Christmas tree would be delivered soon. The doorbell rang and I opened the door to see two men holding a tree that must have been over 10 feet tall – they could hardly carry it. My mother ushered them into the lounge with it. I was so excited – surely we would need ladders to decorate it. I was looking forward to feeling the presents under the tree and maybe taking a sneaky look at a few before the day. The tree took pride of place in the lounge next to a roaring fire. I was concerned that some of the chocolate decorations near the fire might melt, so decided I would have to eat those now!

Christmas Day arrived and I was up early opening my presents. I had tried to stay awake all night to meet Santa and I don't know how I missed him! Wonderful smells from the kitchen were filling the house, and my mother produced a fabulous Christmas dinner.

I remembered how cold it had been in Staffordshire the previous year. Winters were harsh there, and snow lay on the ground for weeks. On some occasions we had to dig ourselves out of the house when a heavy snowfall blocked the back door, but here there was no snow, no frost or ice – I just could not understand it. It was eleven years before I ever experienced snow in Dawlish.

My mother decided our huge house was too big for three, so she advertised locally and a Bed & Breakfast business was born. After a couple of years she decided to use our house as a residential home, and it became one of the first homes to be registered in Dawlish. She had a good rapport with the local doctors who would send patients for convalescence.

I liked the residents very much, they were like grandparents to me. Some of the ladies would sit in the lounge knitting tea cosies and crochet blankets. Even though they were paying to stay with us, my parents treated them as if they were family and made sure they were happy and comfortable, and when they were sick my mother would nurse them.

My mother, who had a stomach ulcer for many years, was later advised to sell the home as her health was deteriorating, so sadly in 1979 it was sold and my parents moved into a bungalow.

Chapter 4

It was our last school day, 28 May 1982, and then we would be set free to start our lives, to seek our fortunes, to become adults.

At 13 the careers officer had visited us and asked us what we wanted to do when we left school. The classmates who were academically gifted had known for years that they would become pilots, surgeons or genetic engineers. I had wanted to become a nurse, but realised that I would not be able to pass enough exams to enrol in nursing college. I wished then that I had listened to my parents when they used to tell me to try harder, but at that age you just want to be young and free. The human brain is a complex organ; at 13 some brains are not fully developed and are not always capable of storing and archiving large amounts of information – this is something that I realised when I was much older. So at 13 I enrolled on a Pitman secretarial course which I attended once a week after school. A career as a secretary was now my chosen path.

It was lunchtime and we all assembled in the main hall. Disco music was playing and there was plenty of food. The leaving party had both a happy and a sad feeling to it – we were happy to be leaving and to be setting off on our amazing journeys, but sad that we would not see some of our classmates and teachers again. I had a special fondness for my drama teacher Mr Griffiths. His style of teaching was very different from the other teachers at the school: he interacted with the pupils and he brought the best out in everyone. Teachers like him were worth their weight in gold. To my mind he should have been acting on the big screen, he was so talented.

By 3.30 the room was almost empty, this once crowded, noisy room now held a handful of classmates who were reluctant to walk through those doors for the last time, knowing their lives would change forever from that moment on.

It was Friday night, and I was getting ready for the weekly disco. It was the days of the New Romantics, Duran Duran, Human League, Depeche Mode, with their odd hairstyles, and batwing white shirts. All the girls were wearing the latest fashion: tartan miniskirts, black fishnet tights, big hair and lots of eyeliner.

I had butterflies in my stomach, that awful sickly feeling you have when you are in love for the first time, the sweet and sour mix of emotions and feelings. Every detail relating to your love, every smile, facial expression and glance, is recorded in your photographic memory and over-analysed to the point of mental exhaustion.

His name was Richard, and I had met him six weeks earlier. He was from Leyton in East London, and his family had a holiday home where I lived. His mannerisms were characteristic of the London scene, his East End upbringing and accent were a breath of fresh air after the Devonian twang. The gift of the gab, the 'wide boy' image, could have been styled on him. He wore the latest fashion – Gabicci, Fila, Pringle – and smelled divine from expensive aftershave. He was only 15 but looked at least 18.

All my friends thought he was 'It' and I am sure they all secretly fancied him. The local boys were in a different league from him; they really were boys, and he put them in the shade, much to their dismay.

I was stunned that a man actually wrote letters. I wrote to him most days, and he wrote to me every day, sometimes twice a day. I would look out of the window for the postman and could not get to the letterbox quick enough to retrieve my letters. My heart missed a beat every time I opened them, and I would read them over and over again.

I waited outside the disco and at 7 p.m. my best friends Maria and Nicky arrived. We went inside to dance to our favourite song, 'Don't you want me baby'. I looked at my watch every second: it was still only five past seven and I was impatient to go and meet Richard, but the time dragged.

At 8 p.m. I left Maria and Nicky and walked to Richard's house. His father's car was in the drive, so I knew he was here. I ran over to the door and rang the doorbell, my heart pounding so loudly I was sure you could hear it. The door opened and Richard pulled me close to him and kissed me. 'I have missed you so much. I told the old man to put his foot to the metal and get me here.'

15

I went inside and said hello to his family while Richard got his coat, and we headed back to the disco. We walked in, arm in arm, and my friends ran over to say hello to him. It felt as if we had never been apart as I danced with him, and my feelings for him were so strong. I was so happy; I knew I could never be more happy than this. I was unaware that this idyllic happiness would be short-lived and that a week to the day my life would be in turmoil and I would never be the same person again.

We spent the next few days on the beach, soaking up the hot Devonshire sunshine with Maria and her boyfriend and Nicky. Swimming, laughing, being young.

Chapter 5

It was Friday, 4 June 1982. After a long day of swimming I left Richard at 5 p.m. and we both went home for some food. I ate mine quickly. I missed him so much, and we had only been apart for one hour. First love has that effect on you: one hour apart is unbearable. There were never enough hours in the day to be with Richard, every second we were apart felt like years. We had a lot in common; we were both left-handed. He had short blonde hair and deep blue eyes.

Richard wanted to join the Navy, and he was very clever, but was worried that when he eventually applied they would not accept him as he was colour-blind. Like me, he would have to think of another career if this proved to be the case.

I rang the doorbell and Richard opened the door, and as he closed it he slammed it shut. I could tell he was not happy; he had argued with his parents. We met with friends in town; and sat in the park drinking cola and having fun.

By 9.30 p.m. I was getting tired, so I decided to go home. Richard walked me halfway up the hill. He always walked me home, but that night, because he had argued with his parents, I told him to go home and make his peace with them.

He was not happy and said he was walking me home, but I walked off and sent him on his way, telling him I would be okay, I would be home in less than ten minutes, and he was not to worry.

I walked a few feet, and as I turned and looked behind me Richard looked back at me and we waved to each other and blew each other a kiss. My heart missed him so much already.

There was a lane just ahead of me. A man walked from the lane and crossed over the road in front of me and started walking up the hill. I let him get a distance in front of me before I crossed over the road to walk up the hill. As I walked around the corner the man was walking back down the hill towards me. I carried on walking and did not pay much attention to him.

Eventually we were on the pavement next to each other, and as he passed me he asked me if I knew where there was a telephone box (mobile phones had not been invented then). I explained to him that there were three at the bottom of the hill and one at the top. He kept asking the same question, and I could not understand why he did not take in my directions to him, which seemed easy enough to understand.

As I looked at him, out of the corner of my eye I could see that where he had stopped me there was an entrance directly behind me. At that moment I knew he had stopped me to attack me. Fear ran through my mind as the realisation emerged. He also realised at that point that I knew this, and as I moved my feet very slowly to walk away from the entrance, he ran forward and grabbed me. He was so strong that he picked me up as if I was a doll, and ran with me through the entrance.

This footpath was a cliff walk and he pushed me up against the railings. I could feel the spikes digging into my back, and my head was being pushed so far back that I could see the sea below me. I was sure he was going to push me over the cliff.

He had a distinctive look, with brown curly hair, a stocky build, and he was about 5 foot 8. He had a scar on his left cheek. I kept telling myself, don't forget his face, don't forget his face.

I started to scream at the top of my voice, hoping that someone from the houses on the other side of the road would hear me and come to my rescue. But no one came. This place is normally full of dog walkers, but that night there was no one to hear my screams. By now Richard would be almost at the bottom of the hill and would not have heard my cries for help.

The man put his hand over my mouth and told me to stop screaming. His accent was not local, I knew it was a Somerset or Avon accent. The tears were running down my face. After screaming for over two minutes your vocal cords give up on you and your voice is silent. My mind was racing now. With no voice no one would come.

Until that night I was one of the 'It will never happen to me' girls, but now the realisation that I might be about to die was running through my mind. The adrenaline had kicked in and I was trying to keep my mind focused on getting away. I could not rely on anyone to come to my rescue; my actions from now on would determine my fate.

19

The man's first intentions were not to rape me. I supposed he was a loner, a man who found it hard to attract a girlfriend, and I was sure this was why he had attacked me. It was not a vicious attack, he had not hit me, and he spoke calmly and seemed surprised when he asked me why I was crying. A man of low intelligence. A man who I knew was very strong. I had to be certain before I made any move, because it could be my last.

He let go of me and let me come away from the railings, then he forced his face to mine and started trying to kiss me. I felt sick. A stale smell of sweat and unwashed clothes lingered as I tried to push him away. This was my big mistake, an error of judgement that could have proved fatal.

He threw me to the ground with such force that I was lying on my back, and then he was sitting on top of me. He put his hands around my throat and he was squeezing so tight that I was gasping for breath. My life flashed before me. My first thoughts were that I would never see my parents again, I would never get a job or have a husband or family, I would not reach my sixteenth birthday on 16 June, I would die just seven days after leaving school with all my life ahead of me. It was over.

My fear was immense, and my heart was beating so fast I thought I would have a heart attack. Tears were running down my face as I could feel myself slipping away. I had used all my oxygen and my eyes started to close. I prepared myself for death and said goodbye in my mind to my parents. I hoped that they would not suffer too much, that my body would be found intact so that my identification by my gentle mother would not break her heart too much. Maybe one day they would come to terms with this tragedy and be able to live their lives again.

When faced with danger even a juvenile mind can display brilliant logical thinking. A calmness and clearness washes over you, all your senses are heightened, your eyes are bright and take everything in, your ears pick up every sound and your nose registers the smell of your attacker as your body and brain go into overdrive.

I looked into my attacker's eyes, and he looked deep into mine. Surely he knew I was seconds away from dying. He was in a transfixed state, a trance-like look on his face. I tugged at his shirt trying to rip it so I would hold a fragment of evidence in my dying hand so that the police may be able to find my attacker.

I opened my eyes again and he was now leaning forward to add more pressure to my neck. To this day I still do not know how it was not broken. I raised my knees and lunged them into his back, and it was as if a light switch had been flicked. He instantly took his hands from my neck, as if he had been woken up from a dream. He seemed horrified at what he had done to me, and he looked at his hands. He got off me and told me to do what he asked and that he would then let me go.

I knew now that he had his chance to kill me and he had not taken it, so now even if he raped me there was still a small chance that I would leave that place alive.

He started pulling my blouse frantically, like a crazed

21

animal, and ripped it. His hands were now fondling my breasts, his hands were rough and trembling. He then started to pull my jeans off. I was kicking him but his strength was overpowering. Again my fear was back and I was shaking uncontrollably. I did not want him to rape me, and feared that if he did, then afterwards he would decide to kill me. I had seen his face – he knew I could recognise him.

My clothes were thrown into a hedge. I could not believe that not one person had walked along this path. It was not quite dark yet, and he had taken a risk attacking me here in an open area where he could have been seen instantly if someone had come along. I felt I had been here with him for hours, but it was probably only about 20 minutes.

He unzipped his trousers and grabbed my hand harshly. He wanted me to masturbate him. This made me feel physically sick. This stranger had taken me on a journey no women should ever go on.

I touched him, then he pushed me onto my back and tried to rape me. I closed my eyes and prayed it would be over quickly and he would let me go home. I could feel a wet sensation on my leg, and as I looked down I saw that he had ejaculated. A feeling of relief washed over me; he had been so excited that I was saved from the nightmare of being raped.

He got up, dusted himself down, and walked away. His parting comment said it all: 'See you here same time next week.'

I sat on the ground in shock. I could not move. He was only 20 feet away – what if he came back to finish me off? But he was soon out of sight and I looked for my clothes. I put my jeans on and went back onto the main road.

Within seconds a man and woman came walking up the hill. I stopped them and told them I had been attacked – they could see from my clothes and the way I looked that I was telling the truth. They walked me almost to the door and I asked them for their name and address, but they would not give it to me, they did not want to get involved. After all I had been through that night, now my only two witnesses, who could say they had found me, would not help me. This was a harsh blow.

I banged on my front door and my mum opened it. I fell into her arms and cried my heart out. My hair was all matted with grass and I was trying to talk and tell her what had happened, but my voice was still damaged. She knew I had been attacked. I will never forget the look on my father's face when he saw me, a man whose heart was broken. We would never be the same again.

I begged my parents to telephone the police, but they refused. I did not understand why; they would be able to catch him if they looked now, I was sure. I gave my father a description of him and he telephoned his brothers-in-law who went out to find him. I telephoned Richard and told him what had happened. He started to cry, and blamed himself for not walking me all the way home.

I went to my room in the early hours of the morning. I looked in the mirror and saw fingerprints on my neck.

My attacker had left his mark, not only on my skin but also in my mind.

I lay on top of the bed and tried to close my eyes. All I could see was his face looking back at me. The images of him gripping my neck made my eyes fill with tears.

It was not my time to die that night, yet I could hardly believe that I had had this close encounter with death at such a young age, and had walked away with no physical harm, only mental trauma.

The hour hand on the clock did not seem to move. My head was swirling as if I had been drinking, and still I was still saying to myself, don't forget his face.

It was Saturday morning. I had been doing a Saturday job at our local Woolworths for quite some time, but I was so upset that I could not face going to work. I telephoned them and told them I would not be in.

Richard arrived at my house and I went out with him. He asked me what the police had said, and I told him my parents would not let me inform the police. They knew that I would be made to relive this terrible ordeal in a court, if ever the attacker was found, and that the female victim has to prove her innocence to a jury. They knew it would be hard to get a conviction.

I saw Maria and told her what had happened. She was shocked that this peaceful place could have a sexual predator lurking in the shadows.

Until now, apart from the police, I have never told anyone the full extent of the attack. But even now, when I think of that night, it is as clear as if it was yesterday. I can still smell his scent on me. I can still remember his accent, and I still remember that face with its scar. The fact that I survived is almost unbelievable. Things could have been very different: a gravestone, and weekly visits from my parents, flowers to remember a life cut short.

Chapter 6

A week had passed when I arrived home to see a police car outside our house. I went into the lounge, and there were two police officers talking to my mum. My mum and dad had decided that they had done the wrong thing and should have informed the police the night it happened. My mum made us all tea and the two policemen asked me to recall the events of that night. They asked me if I wanted my mum to be present, but because I had not told her the whole traumatic and graphic story I did not want her to be hurt, so I asked if I could talk to them privately.

In 1982 things were very different from today. A policewoman would be present nowadays to ask the intimate details, which are and can be very embarrassing to speak about when you are a 15-year-old girl. I explained to them how it came to be that I was in the wrong place at the wrong time, that he had first tried to kiss me, then became violent when I pushed him away. I was not sure if rape was his initial motivation as it was the last thing he tried to do.

One of the policemen was only in his early twenties and his approach to an assault victim left a lot to be desired. Firstly he wanted to know what clothes I was wearing, maybe a short skirt or low-cut top; this can excite a man, I was told. When I told him I had worn jeans, he then proceeded to ask whether they were tight jeans, as this also can arouse a man. In his eyes, if I had been covered from head to toe in robes I would still have been an object of arousal.

I explained to him that this man did not choose me for any particular reason – if I had walked home five minutes earlier then another poor girl would have been the one he attacked. He had not noticed my clothes at all; I was simply in the wrong place at the wrong time.

It is a well-known fact that most crimes are committed by a person known to the victim, only a very small percentage of all crimes are committed by a stranger. The police officer asked me if my attacker was an old boyfriend, or if I had had an argument with my boyfriend. He implied that maybe I had made up the story for attention.

This comment and accusation made me very angry and upset; this may be the case for a small minority of victims, but not me. I was a victim of a crime. I was the prey, captured by a predatory male, like a lion waiting in the long grass for a lone victim. And now I was made to feel like a criminal.

Police Constable Squires then intervened and reassured me that I had done nothing wrong and said I had been very brave to fight back. He stated that some of the things I had told him I could not have made up.

I was asked the obvious question attack victims are always asked, whether I had an opportunity of kicking the man in his groin. I had thought of this avenue of attack but knew if I had not kicked him hard enough he would have killed me for sure if he had caught me again. I had already seen he had a temper and had managed to cheat death once in the evening. Would I have been so lucky a second time? I think not, and I am sure I would not be here writing this.

Advice is always given to you when you have been involved in any type of incident from 'specialists in the field' and most of this fits into the category of 'could have', 'should have', but when you are facing a life-threatening situation where you are unsure if you will live or die, then you have to make tough decisions.

No one ever knows how they will react when faced with a terrifying situation, we always hope we will be able to cope and will survive. But when push comes to shove, have you got the nerve to see things through to the end and face it head on? When the fear takes over, what will you do? The inner strength in some is not present in others. The journey you are on only has two possible endings – live or die. When your life hangs in the balance and your life flashes before you a sense of life being so precious fills your veins like a narcotic drug.

Amazing stories emerge from tragedies where some people walk away completely unscathed, yet others pay with their life. Is there such a thing as a person who is indestructible, or do we all share the same survival rate, our nine lives?

There is no doubt that your actions in an emergency can greatly improve your overall chance of survival. A misinterpretation of the situation or a wrong choice can determine your fate.

Some advice I can give any women who reads this, which was given to me by Police Constable Squires, is that if ever you are attacked, never shout 'Rape!' or 'Help!', as no one will come to your aid. I am living proof of this fact. Shout 'Fire!' and you will be inundated by helpful bystanders eager to help you. This advice came too late for me.

The police asked for the clothes that I was wearing on the night. My jacket had indentations from the spiked railings, and grass stains; my blouse was ripped; my jeans may or may not have had the residue of my attacker's semen.

DNA screening was unheard of in 1982, an invention that today puts so many criminals behind bars for the crimes they have committed. If his DNA had been on file, mabye he would have been caught, and stopped from committing any further offences of a sexual nature. I was born in a wrong era when such forensic and scientific tests would have been ideas you might have read about in a science fiction magazine. And nowadays an array of counsellors would have been appointed to my case. I would have been offered an extensive counselling programme and help to get my life back to some sort of normality. But in 1982 I was offered nothing, just left to get on with things.

I had explained to the police that I was sure the man and woman who found me lived on a nearby estate, and said that perhaps if it was mentioned in the newspaper they would come forward.

The local newspaper was given a brief outline of the attack to print. I was still only 15, so my name was not printed. This small town, where crime was minimal (and still is), may now have an attacker within its midst. Was he still here, or had he fled the night he attacked me? It was a question no one will ever know the answer to.

The police told me that the chance of ever catching the man was remote: a week had passed, and he would be long gone from Devon by now.

Chapter 7

Richard, who had been very supportive, had now gone back to London. As the weeks went by I tried to get on with my life, but something inside me had changed; my happy-go-lucky approach had gone, my smile had vanished.

I started a six-month Youth Training Scheme as a receptionist at a doctor's surgery in a nearby town. It was good to be busy and the hours in the day did move more quickly when I had something to focus on, but at night when I was all alone in my room the images of the attacker would come flooding back. Sleep deprivation was commonplace, I would wake up in the night in terror, my heart racing so fast. It was a nightmare I could not explain.

One afternoon while I was working, Police Constable Squires visited me. The police had a suspect in custody at Newton Abbot Police Station and they were quite confident that he was my attacker. He was a known rapist and had already been convicted of rape.

I entered a room with two police officers, and saw a man standing in front of me. He was tall, at least 6 feet. He had a shaven head and was very thin, and from where I was standing I could not see any visible signs of a scar on his face.

I had never seen a criminal before, let alone been put in a room with one with only 6 feet of floor space separating us. Today he would have been put in a room and I would have viewed him through a one-way mirror so that my identity was protected.

The police officer asked me if this was the man who had attacked me. I replied that it was not. With that, the man said, 'Thanks love'. I was not going to accuse a man of attacking me if he had not, I hoped that one day the woman he had raped would be standing in my place and she would be able to say yes.

This was an ordeal I could not quite believe I had been made to go through. It was frightening, and no care for me as a victim seemed to enter into anything. I was taken away from my job at a moment's notice, and at no point was I informed that I would be in the same room as this man. I can only imagine what I would have gone through if it had been my attacker.

I asked the police officers why they thought their suspect was the man who had attacked me. I had given my statement so many times, yet they had shown me a man at least 4 inches taller, with a shaven head, who looked like he had been on a starvation diet, and had no scar. The police officer informed me he could have cut his hair and lost weight. I replied that he could not have grown 4 inches and lost a scar!

I went home feeling deflated. After hours spent at a police station, the only suspect they had ever found was nothing remotely like my description.

I was beginning to think that the police either could not read, or were of the opinion that victim's statements are always going to be inaccurate. It is always best to give a statement for a crime as soon after the event as possible so that the facts remain fresh and do not become distorted. On some occasions events recalled at a later date can be slightly different from your first perception of them. I have always had an excellent memory and accurate recall; I knew what I saw, and I knew it was accurate.

Richard came to visit me a few weeks later. I still loved him very much but found it difficult to have any physical contact with him; when he tried to kiss me I would freeze. I could not get that night out of my head, and it was affecting our relationship.

It is hard on loved ones when something like this happens. Sometimes the victim does not realise that they too have been affected by the events, not in the same way as the victim, and they will not feel the same pain, but they do feel pain in a different way. It is hard for them to come to terms with the fact that a stranger has hurt the woman they love.

A boyfriend, husband, father or brother will all share the same feeling – they want to find the attacker. And many that do will take the law into their own hands.

As for the victim, your trust in men can be wiped out in an instant. Most men are not attackers, but they become tarred with the same brush. Only a small percentage of the male population become predators, but when a woman has been attacked then her initial instincts are to protect herself from harm, and the best way to do this is to avoid all male contact. In doing so you accomplish your aim but also make yourself a recluse and in some cases a man-hater.

It is hard to adapt to a relationship when you have been attacked, and things do have to move at the woman's pace. A misconception held by most is that eventually, in time, you will be the same person as before. You will never be the same person again.

I was no longer with Richard. The distance was a problem, and I was finding it just as difficult as in the beginning to trust a man completely. He told me I had become a different person. This was true, I had. It was no fault of my own and I was trying to be the person I had once been, but the events had changed my life and I could not go back.

A person who has never felt the effects of being attacked can never know how life-changing it can be; they will never know what pure fear is all about; they will never know how it feels to know you are going to die. These terrifying situations leave deep mental and physical scars.

The only thing I seem to have benefited from since being attacked is a heightened sense of danger. I have been in certain situations where to the onlooker everything seems calm and normal; they have not noticed anything out of the ordinary. My senses, on the other hand, are able to pick up minute details and evaluate a situation before most are aware of it. It has made me an excellent judge of character, and I can spot a conman and a man who is up to no good instantly.

I was offered a job in a local solicitor's office after I finished the YTS, I was still trying to get on with my life.

A few weeks later I received a telephone call from the police to say I was going to be taken to a pub in Torquay with a plain-clothes police officer; they were confident that a man who used this particular pub was my attacker.

I sat in this pub for a couple of hours, and the officer sat a few seats away from me. I was to cough loudly if the man in question, when he arrived, was my attacker. The evening came and went, and no one I recognised came into the pub at all. It had been another wasted journey, and the police officer said the man they had suspected had not showed up.

Chapter 8

It was now 15 months since I had been attacked, and a friend called Alison had invited me to a party in Torquay. Maria had split from her boyfriend and I too was now single again. I had not really socialised much since that night. I needed time to adjust after the split with Richard. We had been together for just over a year. But I decided it was time to get out there again. I was only 17 and did not want that night to ruin my whole life. It was time to move on.

We all arrived at a large house. Alison went to Torquay College, and the house was full of students.

I was sitting on the floor and wrote some words in German on a piece of paper. I had been studying a home course for a few weeks and was just practising.

A boy came over to me and saw the note and said he was German and his name was Thorsten. He asked if I was German too.

He was very good-looking, very tall with white-blond hair and piercing blue eyes. I liked him instantly. I explained that I was not German, but was learning it. We talked all night and I found out that he was a few months older than me. As we said goodbye, he asked me for my telephone number.

The following day the telephone rang and it was

Thorsten. He asked me out on a date and we arranged to meet the following day. He lived in Paignton so I decided I would catch the train and meet him there.

When the train pulled into the station the first thing I could see was a shock of blond hair: it was Thorsten. We went to a local café and had tea. He had a perfect English accent, no trace of the guttural German I expected. His parents were both German and he had been raised in Hamburg but had moved to England when he was eight years old after his parents divorced. His mother had met and married an Englishman while in Germany, and moved here to be with him.

It was good to be out on a date. For so long I had been in turmoil and did not know what life had in store for me. I knew it could not get any worse than the last year, so was hoping that now things would start to get better.

Thorsten was very open and honest with me; he had only ever had one girlfriend but that was a holiday romance which only lasted a few weeks. I did not know what to tell him about me. After all, was this going to be a one-date wonder? If so, then why burden someone else with my story? He may or may not have wanted to see me again after today. If I poured my heart out to him, what effect would that have? He might head for the hills, or even worse, show the sympathy card. I wanted to have a relationship with a man who would not see me as someone who needed saving and protecting: I had already saved and protected myself. I needed someone who would want to be with me because I was me, to take on board my emotional baggage, and give me strength and comfort, and above all love.

I was now in unfamiliar territory. I had never thought before how I would deal with this situation, although I should have known it would arise eventually: I would meet my soulmate and have to tell my story. This is when I realised how alone I was, and how alone I had been, having no one to share these feelings with, no counsellor to telephone and ask advice. What was going to be my next step, I did not know. I sipped my tea and explained to Thorsten that we had only just met, and it was early days, and if we continued to see each other then I had a few things he needed to know about me.

I was surprised by his reaction. He just said, 'I am not a nosey poker and I don't want to pry. It is good to spend time with you. Tell me when you are ready.' I corrected his English and told him it was 'nosey parker', without trying to sound like a school teacher. I was relieved and felt I had been worrying unduly, but also realised that one day soon I was going to have to tell him. I would need to think very carefully how to go about it.

How much do you tell your boyfriend? Do you tell them the whole stomach-churning ordeal or do you give him a sanitised version, missing out certain parts? After all, I didn't want to put him off. It is difficult to see things from a male point of view; how does a man think or react to this kind of news? This is something I would never know. Giving too much detail may be too much for him to cope with; would he look at me differently from that moment on? Keep me at arm's length or stifle me with affection and not let me out of his sight? Neither scenario seemed particularly appealing to me. If I did not tell him the whole story and played it down as just a minor blip along life's long and winding road, then if he found out the truth later he would feel hurt that I had not trusted him enough to tell him what I had been through.

I decided to sleep on the matter and give it a lot of thought before I told him anything. Maybe I was spending too much time thinking of something that may never arise. We may only see each other for a few dates. That made sense, I told myself: I will tell him in a month if we are still together.

Chapter 9

The days now were full of hope and joy for me. I had a gorgeous boyfriend, I was enjoying my job, my smile was back. I had turned a corner and realised that sometimes life is unpredictable and when you have reached rock bottom there is only one way to go and that is up. My ordeal had made me a stronger person and now I never worried about small things. I had been so close to losing my life that now every second of every day was precious. The girls in the typing pool were worrying that they had split ends or had put on 3 pounds, but to me these were were not worth even thinking about. I had this secret, and wondered how they would react if they knew that this bubbly 17-year-old who was high on life was the luckiest person on the planet, had stared death in the face and walked away unscathed. I felt like I had won the Pools.

This pedestal you put yourself on, as 'The Untouchable', has a downside: it is hard to keep your feet on the ground, you feel that you are invincible, nothing can touch you now – you have survived and you would survive again. The odds of this are miniscule, but some go on a self-destruct mission, living life in the fast lane. I needed to keep my feet firmly on the ground.

It was now week three into my relationship with Thorsten, and I was really beginning to like him. I still had not told him anything substantial about me but knew that I would need to tell him soon. Little did I know that the time would be now. I had not prepared what I was going to say, but things were taken out of my hands.

My mum had invited Thorsten for tea, but as we sat down to eat the telephone rang. I answered it and a voice asked for me; I confirmed who I was. The police officer on the other end of the phone gave me the news that Police Constable Squires had died. I could not believe it. He was not just a policeman to me, he had become my victim support, my belief in justice, and that one day we would find my attacker. How could a good man just die? I dropped the phone and could not speak. My mum took the receiver and talked to the policeman.

The man who had sat in my lounge comforting me and telling me it would be all right had now lost his life. Is that what happens, I lived and now someone else dies in my place? Is that how the scales of life balance out? But why him? It should have been my attacker, not PC Squires.

He was such a nice man, very caring, he had been so supportive to me and without his advice I am sure my recovery would have been much longer and harder to deal with.

Maybe because he had a daughter of his own he had understood how badly it affected me, and as a parent knew how he would feel if his daughter had told him that she had been attacked by a man.

Thorsten kept asking what was wrong and why the police were telephoning me. What had I done? Was I in trouble? I took him upstairs to my bedroom and told him my story.

As I lifted the lid off this box of secrets the tears were running down my face, I was reliving the nightmare again as if it had just happened. The room was silent, and time stood still. Thorsten's face was ashen as for a few moments he looked into space, then he took my hand in his and looked deep into my eyes. 'You lived so I could find you. Your story is now my story. I love you.' He pulled me into his arms and held me so tight. I had not known until now what I was looking for in a relationship, but now I knew: sometimes all a girl wants is to be held tight and told that everything will be okay, that is all. I felt different now I had told Thorsten. In a way he had been the counsellor I never had; he listened to me and never judged me.

My parents blamed Richard for what had happened to me and could not see that it was my mistake, not his. We would all like to live our lives with the benefit of hindsight guiding us to make the correct decision always, but life isn't like that. When any tragedy happens, human nature always wants a scapegoat and someone to blame, but we all have our own responsibility for our safety. It is not any one else's job to keep us safe, it does not matter how careful you are. If it is your day to have your life turned upside down there is nothing you can do to prevent it.

The way that friends deal with a situation shows their true colours, and quickly you become aware of personality traits you had not witnessed before. 'Birds of passage' acquaintances have short memories for events that have no real impact on their own lives; after all, they are free to carry on with their daily lives completely unaffected – the pain is not theirs, it is someone else's.

Within six weeks of my attack the so-called friends who had telephoned and visited me vanished off the radar, and I became the forgotten victim. No one wants to spend time with someone who is always sad or upset; the only way I can explain it is that it feels like a grieving process for when someone dies. After a time of mourning you try to make the best of things, but I had no body to bury, I was grieving not for a person who had died but for my smile, for the person I had once been. She was gone forever and was never coming back; this stranger had robbed me of my spirit.

True friends show their nature also; you are never in any doubt that faced with any problem they would always support you, and this was true of Maria and Nicky. They always say that three is a crowd, but for us three it was just fine, most of the time we were together, growing up. Nicky was a little more serious than Maria and I, and we needed someone to keep us in check. Nicky was in our class at school and we met her when we were about eight. She is a good friend to us both. There has always been an unspoken bond between Maria and me; our lives have been entwined since we were five and there is nothing I would not do for her. She is my female soulmate. I think everyone needs one of them, that special friend that is in your heart; she is the sister I never had.

I continued working, and Thorsten was offered a place at Bristol University. We spent the weekends together, when I would travel to Bristol on a Friday night after work or he would come home to Paignton.

Thorsten was very different from Richard. The first moment I saw Richard the spark was there; he had an illuminating personality, you could never be bored when you were with Richard, he was just a fun guy. I think everyone has a special place in their heart for their first love.

The first time I met Thorsten there was no electrifying spark – well, not for me at least. He had a kind face and a gentle voice and I think I needed that from him. You cannot always be living on the spur of the moment, sometimes you have to be serious about life. I realised after a few months that without a spark that is bright, not just a slight flicker, a relationship can fade away. The spark has to be there from the first moment: it does not appear later, it is an immediate rush of attraction, it cannot be cultivated like a flower to make it grow, the spark is what gives you the love. Without the spark, the love is not deep.

The months turned into years and deep inside I knew that Thorsten was not my soulmate. I think I had used him as a comfort blanket, like an old pair of comfortable slippers to ease me back into having a relationship. I did not realise until this moment that I had become a person that had used another. I did not do this with intent or malice, my young unconscious mind had led me there.

I visited Thorsten in Paignton and ended our

relationship. As I walked away from his parents' house I felt empty. He was looking from the window, and waved goodbye. It took me back to the night Richard had waved goodbye, before the night's events unfolded.

Thorsten knew too in his heart that the course of our time together was run. There were no winners and no losers in this race, both of us had now grown up. I would never forget him, and the support and love he had shown me, and we said we would remain friends.

Chapter 10

The post had arrived. I went to the letter box and there was a long, cream-coloured envelope with an expensive feel to it. I wasn't expecting anything but I opened it.

Inside there was an invitation: Maria was getting married. I was so excited at the thought of attending this wedding. As I read the card my mind was back at the bottom of the hill on my scooter, the day we met, and realised we would be friends forever.

We both worked in the same town and still saw each other regularly; even though our paths were different occasionally they would cross, and we could telephone each other and talk as if we had never been apart.

She is half Greek, and a beauty queen if ever I saw one and I knew her father would put on a show for his lovely daughter. And what a wedding it was. Traditional musicians from Cyprus were flown in, a Greek Orthodox priest performed the ceremony, and her father impressed us all with his Greek dancing. They really knew how to throw a great party. She had so much money pinned to her dress that she walked away with quite a few thousand that day. She shone with radiance like a star, with her olive features inherited from her father, and her dress was breathtaking.

Nicky was next, and as before a letter arrived one day, an invitation to her wedding. She too was beautiful in her stunning dress, with her tall, swan-like elegance.

Chapter 11

Then a sadness like no other was upon me. I was 23 at the time, and the pain I suffered the night of the attack was nothing compared to this pain. My father had been diagnosed with cancer, and within three months he would be dead.

My father had not been to the doctor at all while he had lived in Devon, so when he felt ill the doctor thought his medical records had been mislaid or lost, as there were none!

It was too late for him to receive any treatment, only pain relief was prescribed. This illness strikes the healthy and ravages them, a strong man soon looked like a skeleton.

I remember reading the notes left by the nurse that visited daily to administer my father's intravenous morphine dose, she wrote that he was anorexic. Anorexic due to the fact that he could not swallow food or keep anything in his stomach without being violently sick; he had become anorexic as a secondary illness to cancer, not the other way around.

This gentle lovely man who had a good heart and always supported the underdog suffered so much pain it broke my heart to see him.

I was now working as a secretary locally, and I was

so worried that one day while I was at work he would die before I could get home to say goodbye to him. I could not get home quick enough to spend my hours with him. I knew there would not be many more days and I treasured every moment. His little dog Max sat on his lap all day to keep him company; animals have a sixth sense, and he knew my father was dying.

Sometimes, knowing that someone is dying can be worse than an instant death. You have the advantage of trying to come to terms with the inevitable, and you also have time to devote your time and affection to that person, but this is a double-edged sword: weeks or months of knowing the end result, that you have no control over, can destroy you. You start to wonder why did you not notice they were ill, then maybe if a doctor's intervention had taken place sooner, a cure could have been found. Another scenario placed in the 'could have', 'should have' archive.

An instant death is exactly what it is, no time to say goodbye or to make plans in advance. A shock for the immediate family and friends, but for the victim I think a kinder way for them to die. Maybe they feel pain at the time of death but it would be short-lived, or if they die in their sleep then this is the most painless and nicest way for them to go.

He died at home with my mother and I with him, and as he took his last breath we were both holding his hand. It was a surreal experience. To watch your father, the greatest man on earth, close his eyes and leave you forever is a hard sight to see.

We always called him Sunny Jim because of his

smile. My wonderful, loving dad, who was the kindest of men, had lost his fight. But now his pain was over, no more suffering from this invasive, destructive illness. He was free.

As I looked around the church at his funeral, full of friends and family, my feelings turned to our arrival in this town when I was five. My father loved life so much. He was impatient to reach 60 so that he could retire; he planned to travel and explore more of Devon with my mum. Sometimes when you wish for something too much you do not get it, and he died at 58.

As we closed the door at my mum's house after the last of the relatives had gone, a sadness filled the room. It was just me and Mum now.

It can be tough when you are an only child; with siblings they can share some of the responsibility of caring for the parents, but when there is only you, everything is on your shoulders. As the parents get older a role reversal seems to take place. What day week or month this happens we never seem to notice but one day you become the parent and they become the child.

A big family is wonderful; all my aunts and uncles were lovely, and when we were all together it was a special time. A large family also brings much sadness with numerous church services, not for weddings but more for funerals as another member of your gene pool passes away.

After my father's death my Uncle Ken was always at hand if my mother or I needed anything. A problem with the car, a leaking sink and he would down tools and come to our rescue.

Until now I had never really been interested in learning to drive, it just did not appeal to me. My father's car was sitting in the garage and my mother did not want to see a stranger driving it. I decided to learn to drive and then at least for now I could drive it.

Chapter 12

I tried, at least for a few hours a day, to put these sad events to the back of my mind and concentrate on my work. I knew by working I could earn money and eventually be able to travel – today that is my passion, it is my drug.

I was shopping one Saturday afternoon and was trying to reach something from a high shelf. I was already on tip-toes but needed another couple of millimetres then a hand appeared from nowhere and lifted it off the shelf for me.

He was 6 foot 2, I was 5 foot $1^1/2$ (the half is very important when you are vertically challenged like me). He was smiling and was quite proud of the fact he had been my Knight on a White Charger saving the day. I did not have the heart to tell him that I was going to ask the tall man on the grocery section to help.

His name was John and he was very cute and there was a spark between us and a twinkle in his eye. He looked very different from Richard and Thorsten, who were both blond; John had short dark hair and an Italian look about him.

He asked if he could be of further assistance, perhaps as a personal shopper for me. I liked that idea, but instead I gave him my telephone number and invited him to call.

A few days later the telephone rang and it was John. We arranged a date. He was really good company, there was something about him that I liked, and he made me laugh all the time, something I had not done in a long time. In love you have to have the spark, but also it is important to have a partner who can make you laugh and he certainly seemed to have a happy disposition.

He told me about his family. His grandfather had sold fruit and veg in London. His stall had been next to J. Sainsbury and they were great friends. He was of Italian decent and John looked just like him.

As the evening wore on I knew he was going to want to know all about me; I was back on the roller-coaster, not knowing whether to stay on or jump off. Now I had another story to tell, the death of my father. They say that things happen every seven years, hence seven years bad luck, and this seemed to be running true for me: my father had died seven years after I had been attacked.

The questions arose in my head again: What do I tell him? When do I tell him? Do I tell him all of it in one hit like a one-night performance of a play, or spread it out like a weekly soap? Telling him all of it may leave him feeling like he had just completed a marathon as the only runner – not a relay where he could pass the baton. Telling him in instalments may make him wonder how many stories I had waiting in the wings. After telling him, what would his reaction be? I could not hope for the same response that I received from Thorsten – or could I? John was a chilled kind of guy, I may have misjudged him.

One scenario I had not thought of until now was that he may think that being with me was incredibly bad luck. Some people will only experience one tragedy in their young lives, but I had already experienced two, so was there a pattern forming? Was I a modern-day witch or just an unlucky person whom fate had dealt a couple of bad hands?

The night had been good fun, and it was time to go. John had picked me up from my house, so he drove me home. I really liked him a lot, and we arranged to meet the next day.

John worked with his family who had recently purchased a business when they moved from London to Devon. After a few weeks I met his family, who were very nice, and he met my mum. I had decided that after he had met her I would sit him down and tell him my story.

His first question to me after we had left my mum's house was where was my dad, and this gave me the opportunity of answering him without bringing the subject up myself.

I started to explain to him about my father dying, and he looked sad. I thought I would strike while the iron was hot and tell him about the attack. It all came flooding out as it had before when I was telling Thorsten, but this time I had no tears, no emotion. It was as though I was telling him about someone else's life, not mine. After I had told him I made a joke, and told him if he wanted to leave while the going was good then now was the time.

John had a different reaction than I imagined he would: he was angry that I had been hurt, and he was not happy that Richard had not walked me home. We were both only 15, I explained to him. No one could have predicted that I or anyone else would have been attacked, not in my little town, but it happened, and that was that.

I was pleased that I had told him everything. Most people have small things in their past to tell, a few insignificances that are neither here nor there in the grand scheme of things. I had had lots of sleepless nights over the last few years and didn't want to have any more, worrying about the impact my story may have on someone else. I can only be honest and truthful, and if someone does not want to be with me because of my past, then I cannot change that.

Chapter 13

I was preparing dinner and looked at the clock in the kitchen. I was sure John had told me he was coming over tonight for dinner, but he was really late. I was just about to call him when the door opened. It was John. 'Shut your eyes,' he said, so I did.

He lifted my left hand and I felt the coldness of metal slip onto my finger. I opened my eyes and saw a beautiful ring on my finger. With that, John fell to the floor on one wobbly knee and said, 'Will you marry me?' Without hesitation I said yes.

I was completely astounded and surprised, I had never thought anyone would want to marry me. I would say I am attractive, and I do get the odd wolf whistle, but I'm not a beauty queen or a catwalk model by any stretch of the imagination. For the first time, someone wanted to be with me for me; they had nothing to gain by being with me, I had nothing to offer a man, only my heart which was a little cracked in places but not completely broken.

I telephoned my mum, who was so happy, she really liked John. We had a small engagement party for family and friends and started planning our life together.

I lived in my flat in Dawlish and John had a flat in Torquay, I decided to sell my flat and move in with

John until he could sell his flat, then we would buy a house together.

It was an exciting time, planning the wedding. Those days brought some happiness back into my life. My father would have liked John – my father liked everyone. Now I had no one to give me away when I got married; but then I had the answer – an obvious choice was my Uncle Ken, he had no children of his own and would never have had the chance to walk down the aisle, so I asked him and he was thrilled.

The wedding was planned for 25 June, with a honeymoon in Hawaii. My mother and John's mother went with me to Exeter to buy a wedding dress. It was beautiful, off-the-shoulder ivory satin, with a figure-hugging waist. I felt like a princess in it.

I was working with John and his family in their business at the time, and life was good. Christmas was spent with my mum and his family and everyone was getting excited about the wedding in six months' time.

On our way to work one morning we stopped off at John's mother's house. His mum asked me to telephone my mum urgently, as my uncle had died. One of my father's brothers had been very ill, so I was expecting that maybe he would pass away soon.

I telephoned my mum and the conversation was mixed up and strange. She was at my aunt's house in Dawlish, but I could not understand why she had gone there as my uncle lived in Staffordshire. Perhaps Mum was so upset that she had visited my aunt who lived close by. Then something she said brought me back down to earth and the horror of the story became apparent. It was my Uncle Ken who had died. I screamed the place down. Not my Uncle Ken! No, not him!

We were all devastated. The next few weeks were a blur and I do not remember eating or sleeping. A light had gone out in our hearts.

After a month of sadness I told John I wanted to postpone the wedding. I could not get my mind or heart into arranging a wedding. I had no one to give me away now. I had an uncle in Staffordshire who I could ask, but I felt bad as he had not been my first choice.

John and I started arguing all the time about any small thing. He thought I did not want to marry him. I did, very much, just not at that time – maybe later in the year. He just did not understand this and was pressurising me to get married. He was very supportive at first but he had never lost any family member, and carried on with his life completely unaffected.

The arguments got so bad that one night I packed my things and left John's flat. I had lost weight and was heading for a nervous breakdown if I did not go. I knocked on the door and my mum gave me a hug. As always, she was there to wipe away my tears.

For the next few months John repeatedly telephoned me, but I avoided him. If I did not answer the telephone he could not speak to me. Sometimes you cannot go back, you have to keep moving forward.

Chapter 14

I was now homeless, and jobless too as I had been working with John's family. My mum said I could stay with her as long as I needed to.

I had to dust myself down and try to rebuild my life for the third time. At this point in my life I was feeling very low and depressed; it was hard to keep focused when something seemed to be waiting to bring me down. How much pain can one person take? I was still only 26, yet I had had more to cope with than most people do in a lifetime.

I was happy about one thing: I was back in Dawlish. I love this town, and the beach walk to Dawlish Warren always made me feel good. The sun was shining when I set off for the 3-mile walk along the beach one day. As I looked back along the sea wall I noticed a building development. I made a decision that when I finished my walk I would go and take a look. The developer was on site and he showed me some houses and flats. I liked the look of one of the flats and decided to buy it.

During the next few weeks I went to the Job Centre and applied for jobs in the local paper. I was glad now that I had learned to type, as I found a job in that field very easily.

My friends always told me how nervous they were when they had to go for an interview, but I never felt like that. I am sure that my past has made me have no fear of things I cannot change the outcome of. I was just myself, and my sunny approach must have appealed to the employer as I was offered the job and asked to start the following Monday.

The flat would be ready just before Christmas, so on 23 December I moved into my new home. It was strange being on my own again, but deep down I knew that I only had myself to rely on in this world; I had been forced to grow up quickly.

Mum was coming to stay over Christmas, which was a bitter-sweet time of the year for both of us. Sweet memories of the first Christmas in Dawlish, with the real tree and our new life we had just started, seemed so long ago. The Christmases had always been good until my dad had died; he was ill during Christmas and we were blissfully unaware that it would be his last with us. If only you could go back in time just for one day, maybe to change the course of life or to say the things that are important to your loved ones. Another artefact in the 'could have' 'should have' archive. My Christmases with Thorsten were always full of fun; he had a very young brother who was four when we met, so it was lovely watching him opening his presents as we had all done as children, seeing the excitement in the child's eyes as the paper was peeled off to reveal his dream toys.

This Christmas was a sad, bitter Christmas. I remembered the previous year when I was with John and we were planning our life together. Now I was on my own, thinking of him, and he was on his own; maybe he too was thinking of me if only for a second or two. I still missed him so much and could not see through the haze that found me here single once again and not his wife as I had dreamed I would be.

I am so lucky to have my mum. She is a wonderful mum, a living proof that unconditional love exists between parents and offspring. What inner strength does a parent have when something happens to their child? Is it inherited or is it instinct? What she must have gone through herself during that time must have been terrible. To see your daughter standing before you, her clothes ripped, her skin bruised and mauled by a stranger, must give you nightmares and a pain in your heart you will never get over. A parent's role is to protect you from harm, but what if the danger is not seen, it creeps up on you and strikes so swiftly it is over before you have time to react? A parent is not given a book on how to do the most important job in the world, the only job with a vague job description and no script.

As lunch was cooking in the oven we got ourselves ready and went to the cemetery to lay flowers on my dad's grave and Uncle Ken's too. They both loved life and loved Christmas. My Uncle Brian was also buried near to them; the three of them had spent many hours playing cards, snooker and opening the 'Party Seven'. They all left Staffordshire to start a new life in Devon, and all of them had their lives cut short. Brian was 51 when he died, my dad and Ken were both 58, and they left behind three widows with their own hopes and dreams abruptly ended.

Maybe a new year would be a new start for me. I was hoping for a better year than the one before. Who knows what is in store for us in the next chapter of our lives?

Chapter 15

The new year came and went and I was still working in an office. While I was working one day, my mother telephoned me during my lunch break. A local shop was for sale, a very busy newsagents with various high-earning commissionable products. Six weeks later I was running a shop.

It was a big commitment and a gamble. I had sacrificed a good job and the business's success was now in my hands. If it did not make a profit then I would not be able to pay my mortgage and bills. I had no rich husband or second income to fall back on – it was down to me, and me alone, to make this succeed.

Everything I learned about running a business I learned myself, with no training, I did my own bookkeeping to trial balance and astounded myself; my accountant congratulated me on my exceptionally high standard. Maths was not a subject I did very well at in school, and now to be balancing the books I realised was proof of my theory about my brain developing later.

The winter time was used for planning what we were going to buy for the season ahead. I worked full-time in the shop and had a couple of part-time staff and one full-time, Glenda, who had worked for the previous two owners and had been there for about eight years. She was a bubbly Gemini who was an asset to any business; the customers loved her. In the first few years she was of great help to me steering me away from the hundreds of reps who would try to sell me their wares.

Our customers were wonderful, some had been using the shop for 50 years. Familiar faces would appear every season for their annual holiday, and their first port of call after getting off the train or bus was the shop. I met some wonderful people during my time there.

It was a most enjoyable experience, and the profits increased within weeks of ownership. I had found something I could do. I would never have believed I was capable of walking into a business and running it from day one.

I had not been feeling well for quite a long time and one morning I woke up with a severe sharp pain at the base of my throat. I booked an appointment to see my doctor and she requested a blood test. My doctor's initial diagnosis was correct: I was suffering from hyperthyroidism, an overactive thyroid.

I had been to other doctors on numerous occasions, complaining of headaches and my arms aching when I was washing my hair; also I could hear my own heart beating. These are all classic symptoms of a thyroid condition, I have since discovered, but the doctors I saw said I was probably working too hard in the shop.

I was prescribed medication to stop my thyroid gland from producing any thyroxine. Hopefully my high levels would then fall to the required amount.

I asked my doctor what causes thyroid malfunction.

There are several possible causes. It can be hereditary, but stress or turmoil in your life can also affect it. It is mainly a female illness: 1 in 50 women will develop either hypothyroidism (underactive) or hyperthyroidism (overactive) while only 1 in 1,000 men will develop it.

I explained that I had been attacked when I was 15 and my throat was badly damaged due to strangulation. This could be a possible cause, according to my doctor: early trauma can affect your thyroid function and as you age then it can start to show the effects of the trauma. So I will never know whether the attack caused my illness, or maybe the trigger was a combination of the attack and my father dying.

After six years we decided to sell the shop as my mum's health was not very good and she had come out of retirement to help, so I got another job in an office.

Chapter 16

I met up with Maria for coffee one day, and she was very chirpy. I asked her what she was so pleased about, and she told me there was going to be a school reunion, and more to the point, were the three of us going? We were a bit apprehensive and unsure as to what to expect. Maria and I were not what you would call academic; in fact we had spent most of the time daydreaming and waiting for the bell to ring. The fact that we had achieved anything at all came as a complete surprise to both of us. I am sure it was a fluke!

We decided the three of us would meet in a local pub before to have a couple of drinks for Dutch courage and to discuss our game plan. If we walked in and everyone shouted out 'Not them' we would leave quickly, but if the atmosphere was judged to be calm and accepting, then we would go in.

The three of us waited outside, then we started off walking in three abreast but, just before the doors opened, Maria and I did what we often do and pushed Nicky to the front. She is much taller than us, and we were scared. As the doors opened everyone looked over at us. They all appeared to be smiling and I didn't see any missiles heading our way, so we entered.

I don't know what we were worrying about, seeing

our old classmates was great, and listening to them telling about their lives and achievements. Most of them were instantly recognisable; some had moved away and a few of us stayed in Dawlish. I was asked what I had been up to and whether I had married. I just glossed over my life, as no one in the room apart from Maria and Nicky knew anything about my long and painful journey. After all, it was a night for fun and happy times, not to dwell on events that could not be changed once they had happened.

You never quite know what to expect at a reunion. Will the pupils who you were not friends with talk to you, or will they still hold a grudge? The childish behaviour of children had disappeared now; these adults had put the past behind them and spoke to friends and foes.

The years have gone so quickly. In the blink of an eye 26 years have gone. You feel 16 in your heart and in your head, it is only your reflection in the mirror that shows the passage of time.

My best friends Maria and Nicky have had a different life from mine. Both of them married, and both of them have two children – one boy and one girl each.

As for me, I am still single. I have had a few low-key relationships but no one special in my life. I have drifted in and out of relationships, never taken anything too seriously, never really felt love, just loved to be a free spirit. Geminis are not the best star sign to have a long-term relationship with, they are very flighty, they have a low boredom threshold and need constant stimulation. Maybe there isn't a soulmate for everyone, or maybe I have met him, but fate does not always let you keep your happiness for long. Life seems to be filled with times of great joy, only to be destroyed by moments of immense sadness. But I am not a quitter so will not give up completely on the idea of finding Mr Right just yet.

I travel as much as possible; maybe this form of escapism is what has helped me remain focused. I always seem to be able to 'rest my mind' while I am away; perhaps because I am in another country, the memories of England are far away.

The medinas and souks of Cairo and Marrakech, imperial cities of ancient grandeur, sights beyond belief. I basked in the warm waters of the Indian Ocean while visiting Zanzibar. Scuba diving the Great Barrier Reef and the jewel in Egypt's crown the Red Sea, camel riding in the Sahara Desert, hot air balloon rides above the Valley of the Kings. I travel alone, mostly just me and my camera; my father's words were so true: 'He who travels alone travels the fastest'.

The events of that fateful night are never talked about. Maybe I will be watching a movie with friends and an attack scene is shown. They look at me in silence, and the realisation of what happened, and that it could so easily have been one of them.

I was once asked whether you can really ever be truly happy if you remain single. Some people think happiness is only achieved if you marry and have 2.4 children. My answer is that you make your own happiness, and your own luck. I have been fortunate, and enjoyed a carefree lifestyle. Some of my friends wish now that they had done more for themselves instead of getting married really young, but the feeling of a man's arms holding you tight, and the sound of his voice telling you everything will be okay, is something I do miss.

The memories of that night are still as clear as crystal. I would recognise him now if ever I saw him again. He may not have the same brown hair, it may be grey, and he may have put on weight or lost some, but that face with its scar is imprinted in my brain, never to be erased. I do not hate him for what he did to me, I never have; he had his reasons for why he chose his actions.

He may be a husband and a parent now, on a different life path. I had many nightmares and I am sure he had more than me – he has had to live with himself and come to terms with what he has done; a bad deed done to a person can come back on you. I am sure that his actions that night were of a mixed-up, desperate man who went too far with his own fantasies.

I can still remember my feelings and thoughts as my life flashed before me. Would my life have followed this path if I had not been attacked? I will never know.

I have learned that you have to move on with your life. We cannot change what has already happened, there is no quick fix or drug you can take to speed up the healing process, but time is a great healer. The unbearable pain you once had is now diminished into a dull ache. It is always with you, a gentle reminder that you are not immortal.

Any woman is a target, it does not matter how old you are or what your skin colour is – these things often do not matter to a predatory male. He is looking for his 'thrill ride' and tonight it could be you. Ladies, stay safe!

You can call it fate, a guardian angel, or whatever you like, but someone or something was watching over me, and gave me the strength and courage to survive. That night was not my time to die, it was my time to live. So maybe I am not a victim after all, but a true survivor.